# Foreword

On Monday, October 1st, 1979, an Aer Lingus 747 landed at Logan Airport in Boston, bringing Pope John Paul II on his historic visit to the United States. It was only the second time that a Pope had visited America – the first was in 1965, when Pope Paul VI came to address the United Nations – and it was to be an occasion that will live in the memories of all who took part, however remotely, for many years to come.

Few people would argue that this Pope is quite different from most of his predecessors. John Paul seldom seems to use the weight of his authority but, rather, sets out to impress his message by his own example of Christian faith and common humanity.

The vast crowds that flocked to see and hear him in Boston, New York, Philadelphia, Des Moines, Chicago and Washington, were drawn by his personality, charisma and outstanding quality of leadership, and found in his message an unshakeable belief in the future of mankind. As Bishop Daniel Cronin of Fall River, Massachusetts, explained: "...He's real. The way he engenders enthusiasm, it's as though the Holy Spirit has become visible."

Certainly those involved in his visit shared in a unique experience – an experience that may be relived again in the pages of 'The Pope in America – A Pictorial Record'.

4

### Arrival – Boston

"…America has opened her heart to me. And on my part, I come to you, America, with sentiments of friendship, reverence and esteem. I come as one who already knows you, and loves you, as one who wishes you to fulfill completely your noble destiny of courage to the world."

"…Permit me to express my sentiments in the lyrics of your own song: 'America, America, God shed His Grace on thee. And crown thy good with brotherhood, from sea to shining sea.'

And may the peace of the Lord be with you always, America."

"...To all of you I extend – in the name of Christ – the call, the invitation, the plea: 'Come and follow me.' This is why I have come to America, and why I have come to Boston tonight: to call you to Christ – to call all of you and each of you to live in his love, today and forever. Amen!"

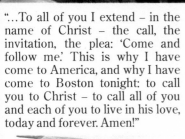

"...I desire to express my gratitude to the General Assembly of the United Nations, which I am permitted today to participate in and to address.

My thanks go in the first place to the Secretary General of the United Nations Organization, Dr. Kurt Waldheim. Last autumn, soon after my election to the chair of St. Peter, he invited me to make this visit, and he renewed his invitation in the course of our meeting in Rome last May.

From the first moment, I felt greatly honored and deeply obliged. And today, before this distinguished assembly, I also thank you, Mr. President, who has so kindly welcomed me and invited me to speak."

"...I hope that the United Nations will ever remain the supreme forum of peace and justice, the authentic seat of freedom of peoples and individuals in their longing for a better future."

## Harlem and Bronx...

"...In this great City of New York, there live a great many immigrants of a variety of colors, races and nationalities, among which is a large community of Spanish-speaking people to whom I now direct myself.

I came here because I know the difficult conditions of your existence, because I know the sorrow that takes place in your lives. For this reason, you deserve particular attention on the part of the Pope."

**Yankee Stadium...**
"...Christ demands openness to our brothers and sisters in need – openness from the rich, the affluent, the economically advanced; openness to the poor, the underdeveloped and the disadvantaged. Christ demands an openness that is more than benign attention, more than token actions or half-hearted efforts that leave the poor as destitute as before or even more so."

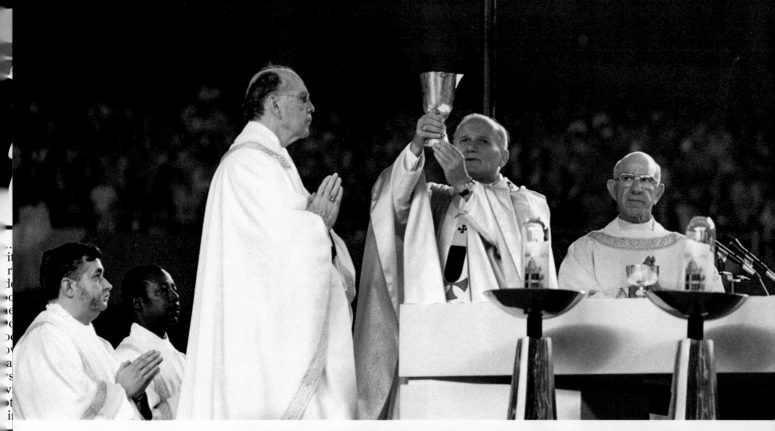

"...And so, in the name of the solidarity that binds us all together in a common humanity, I again proclaim the dignity of every human person: the rich man and Lazarus are both human beings, both of them equally created in the image and likeness of God, both of them equally redeemed by Christ, at a great price, the price of 'the precious blood of Christ'."

21

**Madison Square Garden . . .**
"...Dear young people, you and I and all of us together make up the church. And we are convinced that only in Christ do we find real love and the fullness of life. And so I invite you today to look to Christ.

When you wonder about the mystery of yourself, look to Christ, who gives you the meaning of life. When you wonder what it means to be a mature person, look to Christ, who is the fullness of humanity. And when you wonder about your role in the future of the world and of the United States, look to Christ."

26

27

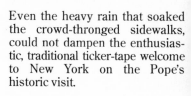

Even the heavy rain that soaked the crowd-thronged sidewalks, could not dampen the enthusiastic, traditional ticker-tape welcome to New York on the Pope's historic visit.

When the Pope arrived at St Patrick's Cathedral at 8.25 am, for a service that had been specially set aside for those whose vocation lies in the service of the church, he was met by eager crowds, many of whom had waited since the early hours of the misty morning.

In his brief sermon the Pope praised the practice of morning prayer as "a joyful communal celebration of God's love in Christ," to the 3,000 priests, brothers and nuns gathered in St. Patrick's Cathedral.

**Shea Stadium...**

"...From Rome I bring you a message of faith and love: 'May the peace of Christ reign in your hearts!' Make peace the desire of your heart, for if you love peace you will love all humanity, without distinction of race, color or creed."

• • •

"Keep Jesus Christ in your hearts, and you will recognize His face in every human being. You will want to help Him out in all His needs: the needs of your brothers and sisters."

"…I pray for you, for your families and friends, above all for your children, for the sick and suffering, and to all of you I give my blessing. May God be with you always."

"...Philadelphia is the city of the Declaration of Independence, that remarkable document, containing a solemn attestation of the equality of all human beings endowed by their Creator with certain inalienable rights: life, liberty and the pursuit of happiness, expressing a 'firm reliance on the protection of Divine Providence'."

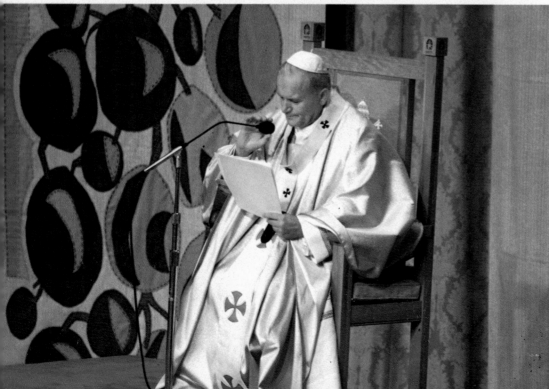

47

es Moines . . .

. .May the simplicity of your life-
yle and the closeness of your
mmunity be the fertile ground
r a growing commitment to
sus Christ". . .was the Pope's
essage from St. Patrick's
hurch, near Cumming, in the
lling farmland of Iowa – his first
op before proceeding to the
apal Mass at Living History
arms, where a gathered crowd
umbered some 350,000 on a
0-acre pasture.

Blue skies and enthuiastic crowds greeted the Pope during his brief visit to Iowa, a stop that was not in the Pope's original itinerary, but was included only five weeks before the tour began, and was the result of a hand-written invitation from a Truro farmer.

## Chicago . . .

"...Brothers in Christ: as we proclaim the truth in love, it is not possible for us to avoid all criticism; nor is it possible to please everyone. But it is possible to work for the real benefit of everyone. And so we are humbly convinced that God is with us in our ministry of truth, and that he 'did not give us a spirit of timidity but a spirit of power and love and self-control'."

"...The Holy Spirit is active in enlightening the minds of the faithful with his truth, and in inflaming their hearts with his love. But these insights of faith and this sensus fidelium are not independent of the magisterium of the church, which is an instrument of the same Holy Spirit and is assisted by him.

It is only when the faithful have been nourished by the word of God, faithfully transmitted in its purity and integrity, that their own charisms are fully operative and fruitful."

**Washington...**

"...We cannot live without love. If we do not encounter love, if we do not experience it and make it our own, and if we do not participate intimately in it, our life is meaningless. Without love we remain incomprehensible to ourselves."

"Thus every one of you needs a vibrant relationship of love to the Lord, a profound loving union with Christ, your spouse, a love like that expressed in the psalm."

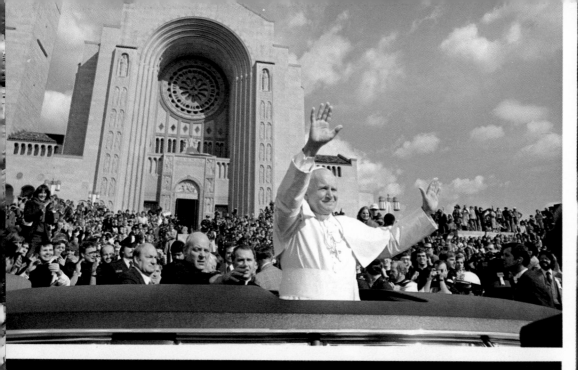

"...Mr. President, I am honored to have had, at your kind invitation, the opportunity for a meeting with you. For, by your office as President of the United States of America, you represent, before the world, the whole American nation. And you hold the immense responsibility of leading this nation in the path of justice and peace."

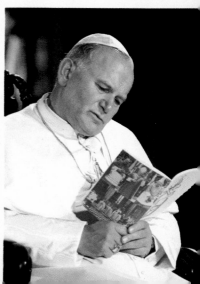

62

"...And now I must leave the United States and return to Rome. But all of you will constantly be remembered in my prayers, which I look upon as the best expression of my loyalty and friendship.

Today, therefore, my final prayer is this: that God will bless America, so that she may increasingly become, and truly be, and long remain, 'one nation, under God, indivisible, with liberty and justice for all'."

God bless America!
God bless America!

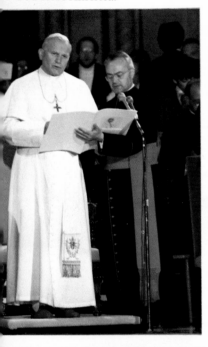